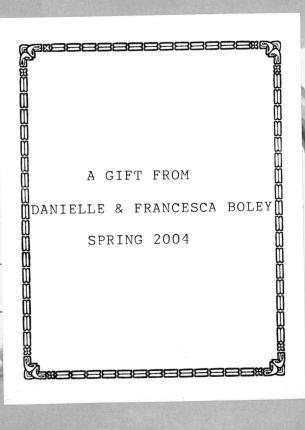

To Charlotte L.R.

To Zak and Ella L.P.

Text by Lois Rock

Illustrations copyright © 1999 Liz Pichon

This edition copyright © 1999 Lion Publishing

The moral rights of the author and illustrator
have been asserted

Published by

Lion Publishing

4050 Lee Vance View, Colorado Springs, CO 80918, USA

ISBN 0 7459 4092 7

First edition 1993

This revised edition 1999

10 9 8 7 6 5 4 3 2 1 0

Acknowledgments

The Lord's Prayer in its modern form as printed in *The Alternative Service
Book 1980* is adapted from the version prepared by the International
Consultation on English Texts (ICET) and is reproduced by permission
of The Central Board of Finance of the Church of England.

Library of Congress CIP data applied for

Typeset in 20/28 Baskerville BT

Printed and bound in Singapore

The Lord's Prayer
for Children

Words by Lois Rock
Pictures by Liz Pichon

LION
Children's Books

Our Father in heaven

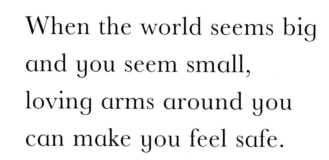

When the world seems big
and you seem small,
loving arms around you
can make you feel safe.

All around you,
all unseen,
is the Maker,
the Great One,
the God who loves you,
child of the world.

Dear God
I am a child:
show me your love.

Hallowed be your name

The Maker of the world
loves big, strong things:
blustery winds,
crashing waves,
towering mountains,
and wild, wild creatures that leap
and run.

The Maker of the world
loves tiny things:
scurrying insects,
nodding flowers,
birds that twitter,
and animals that whiffle and sniff.

The Maker of the world
is greater and wiser
than all these things.
The Maker of the world
is greater and wiser
than anyone.

Dear God
You are greater and wiser
than I can ever be.

Your kingdom come

Some people
like to feel grand
and important.
They like to be noticed.
They speak in a loud voice.
They like to make others
do as they say.

The Maker God is not like that.
The Maker God is unseen,
and speaks quietly
to those who want to listen.

The Maker God
is a gentle king
inviting people to live
in a kingdom of love.

Dear God
Call me to your Kingdom of love.
Call us all.

Your will be done,
on earth as in heaven

If you love others,
you show it in what you do.

You let them have their turn,
their chance.

You forget your quarrels
and become friends again.

You share what you have
so everyone can enjoy good things.

Then the love of the Maker God
shines through you,
and the whole world is a lovelier place.

Dear God
Help me to do the things
that make this earth
more like heaven.

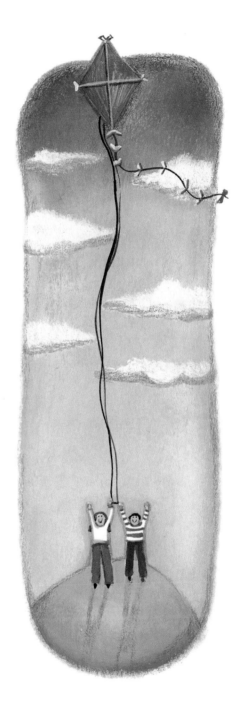

Give us today our daily bread

Here are things
you need each day:
food and drink;
clothes;
a safe place to shelter;
people who love you;

new things to learn;
new things to do;
dreams to dream.

The Maker God wants to give good things to all the people of the world.

Dear God
Please give all your children
good things.

Forgive us our sins

It's so easy to make mistakes,
to get things wrong,
to end up in a muddle.

But think of the sea,
which washes the sand
smooth with every tide.

The God who made the sea
will wash away your mistakes
so every day can be
a new beginning.

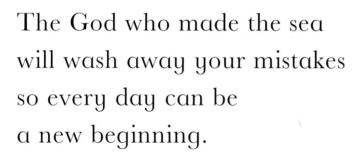

Whatever you do,
the God of love still loves you.

Dear God
Forgive my mistakes.

As we forgive those who sin against us

Sometimes people
get things wrong.

They hurt you.
They make you cry.

But think how the wind
can blow dark clouds away
and let the blue sky be seen.

The God who made the wind
can blow away the hurt
and the sadness
and help you forgive them.

Then everyone can enjoy
sunny days again.

Dear God
Help me to forgive others.

Lead us not into temptation

One path looks hard.
Another path looks easy.
Which path will you take?

The one that leads
to where you want to go!

Sometimes the way
of love seems hard.
The way of selfishness
and spite seems easy.

But the Maker God,
who knows every pathway,
will watch each step you
take and help you choose
the way of love.

Dear God

Show me the way I should go.

But deliver us from evil

The Maker God
taught the birds to make
nests where they can
shelter from the storms.

The Maker God sees
if even one bird falls.
The Maker God
is always watching over you.

Dear God
When bad things are all around,
watch over me.

For the kingdom, the power, and the glory are yours

God is the Maker of all that there is.
Who knows enough words to say
how wonderful is the world?
Who knows enough words to say
how great is the Maker God?

Dear God
Help me to understand
how great you are.

Now and for ever.
Amen.

One day, the world will grow old.
But everything that is love
will be safe with God for ever.

Dear God

Your love will last for ever.

Keep me safe in that great love.

Our Father in heaven,
hallowed be your name,
your kingdom come,
your will be done,
on earth as in heaven.
Give us today our daily bread.
Forgive us our sins
as we forgive those who sin
against us.
Lead us not into temptation
but deliver us from evil.
For the kingdom, the power,
and the glory are yours
now and for ever. Amen.

Our Father, who art in heaven,
hallowed be thy name;
thy kingdom come;
thy will be done;
on earth as it is in heaven.
Give us this day our daily bread.
And forgive us our trespasses,
as we forgive those who trespass
against us.
And lead us not into temptation;
but deliver us from evil.
For thine is the kingdom, the power,
and the glory,
for ever and ever. Amen.

DATE DUE

226.9 Roc   47865
Rock, Lois , 1953-
Lord's prayer for children, The

DATE LOANED	BORROWER'S NAME		DATE RETURNED
8/29/05	BURKE		
2/06			
1-11-11	Mattea		

226.9 Roc   47865
Rock, Lois , 1953-
Lord's prayer for children, The

St. Patrick School
Washington, IL